THE Elvis ALBUM

THE Elvis ALBUM

MILLIE RIDGE

GALLERY BOOKS
An imprint of W.H. Smith Publishers Inc.
112 Madison Avenue
New York, New York 10016

Published by Gallery Books
A Division of W H Smith
Publishers Inc.
112 Madison Avenue
New York, New York 10016

Produced by
Brompton Books Corp.
15 Sherwood Place
Greenwich, CT 06830

ISBN 0-8317-2749-7

Printed in Hong Kong

10 9 8 7 6 5 4 3 2 1

CONTENTS

DEDICATION
To Jonathan, whose musical taste has
always been an inspiration.

The author would like to express her
unbounded appreciation for the help and
expertise provided by stalwart fans Adam
Taylor and Nicholas Sieve.

INTRODUCTION

The life and career of Elvis Presley have been subject to thousands of articles, biographies and fantasies. His songs and films have been alternately derided by critics, or at the other extreme, compared to grand opera and the works of Shakespeare. According to some accounts he lived an unnatural nocturnal existence, his mind clouded by drugs; others say that he was a completely charming man who could not do enough for his family, friends and fans. In life (as in death) he commanded extreme loyalty from those close to him, devotion among his millions of fans, and near-reverence from his fellow musicians. Why?

The secret of his success lay in the early years of his career when his looks, voice and the way he shook his body dazzled one generation, horrified another, and changed the face of popular music forever. This musical triumph was short-lived, but nobody forgot it. In 1958 Elvis was drafted into the US Army and emerged two years later an apparently changed man. The movies he made in the 1960s did not exploit his talents and were a poor replacement for the raw energy of the live Elvis. By the late 1960s the world had begun to wonder what had happened to the King of rock'n'roll.

Presley reemerged in 1968 leaner, fitter and evidently worthy of his crown. It became clear that his future lay in live performances and that is how he spent the remainder of his life, driving the fans wild as he had in his youth. The style of his music altered over the years, but he always managed to belt out 'Hound Dog' with the same conviction that he sang the slower ballads of the latter half of his career. And that is how the world prefers to remember him – as one of the greatest heros of popular music in the twentieth century.

Left: The young King in an early publicity still.

Below: Approximately ten years later he looked just as good in *Spinout.*

Elvis played a variety of
roles during his movie
career, but there were
certain invariables in every
film: singing and girls. He
is pictured above with
Lizabeth Scott in *Loving
You; left,* with Barbara
Lange; *above right*, in
Frankie and Johnnie, and
below right with Barbara
Stanwyck in *Roustabout*.

9

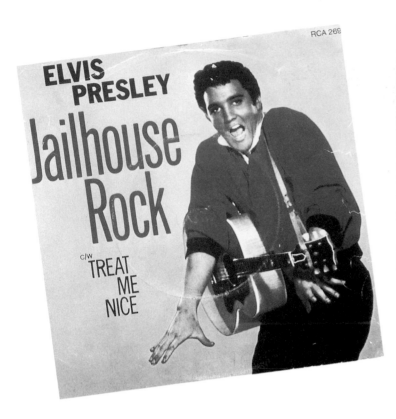

Above: The cover for the single of 'Jailhouse Rock'.

Below & right: Elvis adopts a nautical pose in *Girls, Girls, Girls*

The musical, the amorous, and the pugnacious. *Above:* Elvis rescues a soggy friend watched by a poolside chorus in *Spinout*. *Left:* A classic confrontation in *Wild in the Country*, and a tricky decision arises in *Girls, Girls, Girls* (*top, far right*). Elvis and Ann-Margret boogie in *Viva Las Vegas*, and he takes his punishment on the chin in *Paradise Hawaiian Style*.

Above: One of the many beach parties in the King's musical career, and with one of his younger co-stars, Vicky Tiu, in *It Happened at the World's Fair, (above right).*
Right: Elvis as the sullen Glen Tyler in *Wild in the Country.*
Far right: A classic rebellious pose from the 1950s.

Elvis donned a selection of uniforms, but none quite so bizarre as that in *Frankie and Johnnie (right)*.
Top: As the actor Johnnie Tyrone in *Harum Scarum*, and *(above)* as a navy diver in *Easy Come, Easy Go*. *Opposite below:* With Shirley Maclaine on the set of *GI Blues*, and *above*, in a familiar setting during *Roustabout*.

Elvis was a brilliant entertainer, but he was probably at his best when performing solo. *Right:* Rehearsing for the *Ed Sullivan Show* in 1956; *top left*, in *Double Trouble*; *far left*, in *Tickle Me*, and *Clambake (left)*.
Above: Elvis relaxes with Steve Forrest on the set of *Flaming Star*, and *above right*, takes Ann-Margret for a spin in *Viva Las Vegas*.

1 HILLBILLY CAT

The man who in later life came to epitomize some of the more flamboyant excesses of rock stardom, was born in grinding poverty on 8 January 1935 in Tupelo, Mississippi. The surviving child of twins – his brother Jesse Garon was stillborn – Elvis Aaron Presley was raised by doting parents who lavished affection on their son. Elvis grew up shy, reserved and polite; he had few friends and rarely drew attention to himself at school. By his mid-teens, however, his detachment became more noticeable. Unlike his crewcut contemporaries, Elvis grew sideburns and had a sleek DA; he began wearing distinctive clothes – tight black pants with fluorescent seams – and by the time he left high school he had created a definite image for himself.

Elvis had been given a guitar for his 11th birthday and he sang and played in front of family and friends. His first public performance was at a school concert; he continued to sing well, but no one actually suggested that he should make music his career. When he left school he had little choice but to find himself a steady job, and became a truck driver for Crown Electric, which he enjoyed because he was mad about cars and driving. He was accompanied everywhere by his guitar, and

his now-famous trip to Sun Records in Memphis in 1953 was motivated as much by curiosity to hear how he sounded as by the desire to get an unusual present for his mother. Elvis later described his playing as sounding like 'somebody beating on a bucket lid', but Marion Keisker, the recording assistant, played the tapes to her boss Sam Phillips. He heard in Elvis's soulful voice an unusual blend of gospel and country and western influences. He

Above & left: Home life.
Elvis aged 10, and in 1937
with his parents Gladys
and Vernon.
Right: The boy from
Memphis becomes a star.

Left: The Presley family outside their house in Tupelo, 1942.
Above left: A high school portrait.
Below: Cars became a consuming passion at an early age . . . as did girls, (above right).

introduced Elvis to Scotty Moore and Bill Black, and discovering that they shared the same musical tastes and sense of rhythm, they decided to practise together.

In January 1954 Elvis recorded 'That's Alright Mama' after a session in which Phillips used various production tricks to produce from Presley's voice a sound that would, in time, make grown women weep. By July 1954 'That's Alright Mama' was blowing across the Tennessee airwaves like a hurricane.

At the end of the month Elvis and the boys gave their first live performance. Nervously, Elvis launched into his current hit, playing to a screaming audience who all but drowned his singing. He seemed oblivious to the effect he was creating until he stopped, when he asked the band, 'What's makin' 'em holler so much?'

'It's your leg man . . . the way you're shaking your left leg. That's what got 'em screaming.'

Elvis and the Blue Moon Boys, as they became known, made a huge impact on the South in 1955. They were successful enough for Elvis to follow the well-trodden path of country singers and purchase the first in a long line of Cadillacs; once they had

gained a regular slot on a local radio show, the *Louisiana Hayride*, he was confident enough to give up his driving job. In January 1955 Bob Neal, a local DJ, became their manager and arranged a six month tour through Texas, Louisiana and Arkansas, a series of one-night stands that was crucial to Presley's success. Elvis produced a completely new sound that could not be classified within the old terms of country and western or R & B, so many radio stations were reluctant to play his records. Dazzled by Elvis's frenetic performance, live concerts produced a demand for his records and ensured that he became more widely known.

The catalyst that turned Elvis from essentially a local Southern singer into a national phenomenon was Colonel Tom Parker, a brash promoter whose style of business was unsubtle but effective. The Colonel saw the wild excitement that Elvis generated in his audiences and knew he could turn it to his personal advantage. He became Elvis's manager in August 1955; by November RCA had contracted Elvis from Sun Records and in January Elvis recorded 'Heartbreak Hotel', his first hit. The 'Hillbilly Cat' was well on the way to becoming 'The Nation's Only Atomic-Powered Singer'.

In the early days, Elvis involved his parents in his career and relied on them for advice. He is pictured *above* with his mother and a friend in their Memphis home.

Left & right: Elvis was completely unable to stand still during recording sessions, forcing the engineers to rig two microphones for him.

Right: Elvis wows an audience in California, prompting a reviewer to write, 'Elvis is suffering from itchy underwear and hot shoes.'
Below: A calmer pose, that was no less appealing in the fans.

Far left: A charity concert in Memphis, July 1956. No previous performer had created this kind of reaction, but then Elvis was the only one to possess the unearthly combination of provocative moments and an astounding voice.
Left: A publicity still from the 1960s.
Below left: The price of success. Mobbed everywhere he went, Elvis obligingly signed thousands of autographs in the 1950s.
Below: Elvis rests during a recording session.

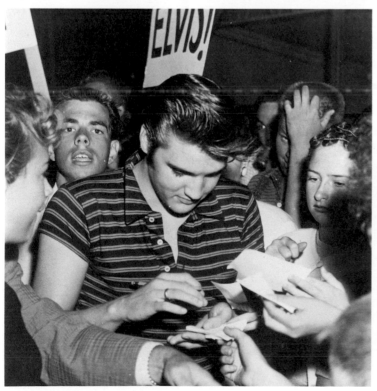

Above: Wearing a shirt better suited to a dentist, Elvis strums during a break in a recording session.
Left & far left: 'If you want to be attractive to girls you should never laugh. You just can't look sexy when you smile'. Or so Elvis thought. Millions of adoring fans disagreed.

Left: Col. Tom Parker, Elvis, Bob Neal and Hank Snow, 21 November 1955, the day Elvis was signed by RCA.
Below: Elvis with his parents on the set of *Loving You.*
Right: Elvis aged 22.

Above: Now a vital part of the legend – Elvis's high school in Memphis.
Left & right: The face that became one of the most famous of the twentieth century.
Below right: Elvis with his manager, Col. Tom Parker, who said, 'I made a bargain with him at the outset. I don't try to sing and he don't interfere with the deals.'

'There's no denying the sheer physical power of this boy. At 21 he gives the impression he has lived for 40 years.' Lizabeth Scott, co-star in *Loving You*. Elvis knew that without his fans he was nothing, so he was rarely shy of press photographers – hence the profusion of photographs of him.

2 FAME AND FORTUNE

Left: A relaxed Elvis chats on the telephone.
Below: Elvis poses for a casual portrait dressed in GI fatigues.
Right: A winning smile from the King as he strums his guitar.

In April 1956 'Heartbreak Hotel' was No.1 in all the music charts. The Colonel had not been idle in promoting 'his boy'; two weeks after his RCA session, Elvis made his TV debut on *Stage Show*, where his 'obscene' performance outraged audiences, and in April he flew to Hollywood for a screen test. It had long been Elvis's dream to become a movie star: 'Singers come and go,' he said, 'but if you're a good actor, you can last a long time.' He performed well and impressed producer Hal Wallis. 'I felt the same thrill I experienced when I first saw Errol Flynn on the screen,' he said, and signed up Elvis with a contract for three films.

In the meantime Presley's music seemed inescapable. RCA was the largest record company in America, but within three months of his initial contract, Elvis's records accounted for more than half of RCA's sales. By 1958, 75 percent of RCA's million-sellers were Presley records, and he was responsible for 25 percent of the company's profits.

1956-58 was arguably the most creative part of Elvis's career. His recording sessions were light-hearted and full of experimentation; the final product was the result of thoughtful playing and editing — music that still sounds somehow spontaneous today. Among the tracks that he laid down in 1956 were classics like 'Don't Be Cruel,' 'Ready Teddy,' 'Rip It Up,' 'Long Tall Sally,' and 'Hound Dog,' which is regarded by many as his greatest hit.

Not only his music seemed omnipresent: Colonel Parker ensured that the public were saturated

Right: Elvis prepares for an appearance on the *Ed Sullivan Show*, 28 October 1956.
Right center: Elvis playing drums in the studio after signing for RCA in 1955.
Far right: Elvis and the Jordannaires pictured in 1956.
Below right: Browsing along the racks of a record shop in Memphis, Elvis checks out the competition, 1957.

with Elvis products, too. The truly devoted fan could have dressed from head to toe in monogrammed Elvis clothing, eaten 'Hound Dog' candy and carried his or her possessions in an Elvis bag. The Colonel's ingenuity in organizing the Elvis souvenir industry knew no bounds. He was driven by a belief that rock'n'roll was a passing craze which would soon fizzle out, and so tried to milk this 'fad' for all it was worth.

After only a year of national exposure Elvis was being hailed as the King of rock'n'roll, a title he assumed after a meteoric career in which he flattened the opposition by producing sounds completely unlike those of his contemporaries.

Elvis's early success was almost entirely due to the radio: he reached only small audiences through his live concerts, did not appear at his best on television, and print articles were usually antagonistic or bewildered about this loud new musical phenomenon. Nationwide television appearances did help the sale of his records, however, although his antics before the cameras aroused such animosity that he was burnt in effigy in St Louis, and petitions were circulated demanding that he be banned from future TV shows. Reviewers seemed to concentrate on the anatomical rather than the musical, the *Journal American* reporting that, 'Elvis Presley . . . makes up for vocal shortcomings with suggestive animation little short of an aborigine's mating dance.' Aware of his reputation, Elvis gave a nervous performance when he appeared on the *Ed Sullivan Show*, nevertheless attracting an audience of 54 million viewers – a third of the nation.

At the height of his success in the summer of 1956, Elvis began filming *The Reno Brothers*. A tale of star-crossed lovers set during the Civil War, the title was changed before the film's release to the more evocative *Love Me Tender*. Elvis was determined to become a good actor and spent long hours watching the movies of Brando and James Dean, hoping to discover the secrets of their skills. Aware that James Dean's death had left a gap for a brilliant young star, Elvis was not the only one who hoped he could fill his shoes. It was unfortunate that Elvis was never really given the opportunity for serious acting, particularly after his return from the army when the quality of his movies declined with the passing years.

Love Me Tender didn't exactly receive unrestrained critical acclaim, but as the *Los Angeles Times* wrote, 'who came to watch Elvis act?' Elvis was at his most appealing in his first movie and he was considered capable enough to receive top billing in his next picture, *Loving You*. This was followed fairly swiftly by *Jailhouse Rock* in the summer of 1957, a film featuring a mean and sullen Elvis as the wild Vince Everett.

By now Elvis was earning serious money and realized he needed a new home to match his status. He had received complaints from neighbors about the fans who hung around the family home on Audubon Drive in Memphis, and their constant presence worried his mother. Graceland was the perfect solution. A large southern-style mansion set in extensive grounds, it became Elvis's retreat for the rest of his life.

In October 1957 Elvis took off on what proved to be his last concert tour until the 1970s. By the end of the month, his album from *Loving You* topped the album charts, 'Teddy Bear' was in the singles' top ten, and the title song from *Jailhouse Rock* had just been released, with the premier of the movie only two weeks away. No other performer (let alone a 22-year-old) had ever had such a concentration of hits at one time. Not surprisingly given the immense publicity, his tour of the Pacific Northwest was a roaring success, despite a near riot in Vancouver and more accusations of obscenity in Los Angeles. Even after 18 months of bump and grind, there were still some sections of American society who couldn't tolerate the antics of 'Elvis the Pelvis'.

Elvis had just started work on his fourth movie when a letter arrived that he, his fans, and his record company had been dreading: Elvis had been drafted. He gained a 60-day deferment to finish filming *King Creole*, and on 24 March 1958 Elvis joined the US Army.

These pages: Several studies of the youthful Elvis as the star who delighted his many fans.

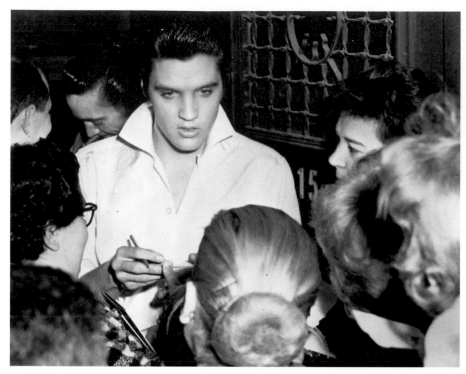

Above: Elvis signs autographs during a break from filming his first film, *Love Me Tender*, 29 October 1956.
Above right: An apprehensive Colonel Tom Parker searches for his protégé.
Right: Elvis with one of the fruits of his stardom.
Below: The King and an early girlfriend, Dorothy Harmony.
Far right: Elvis prepares to leave Graceland surrounded by adoring fans.

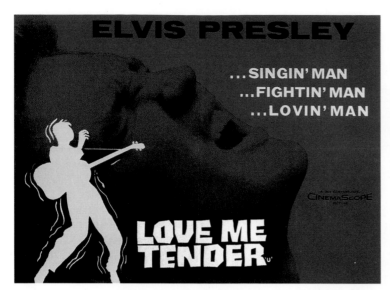

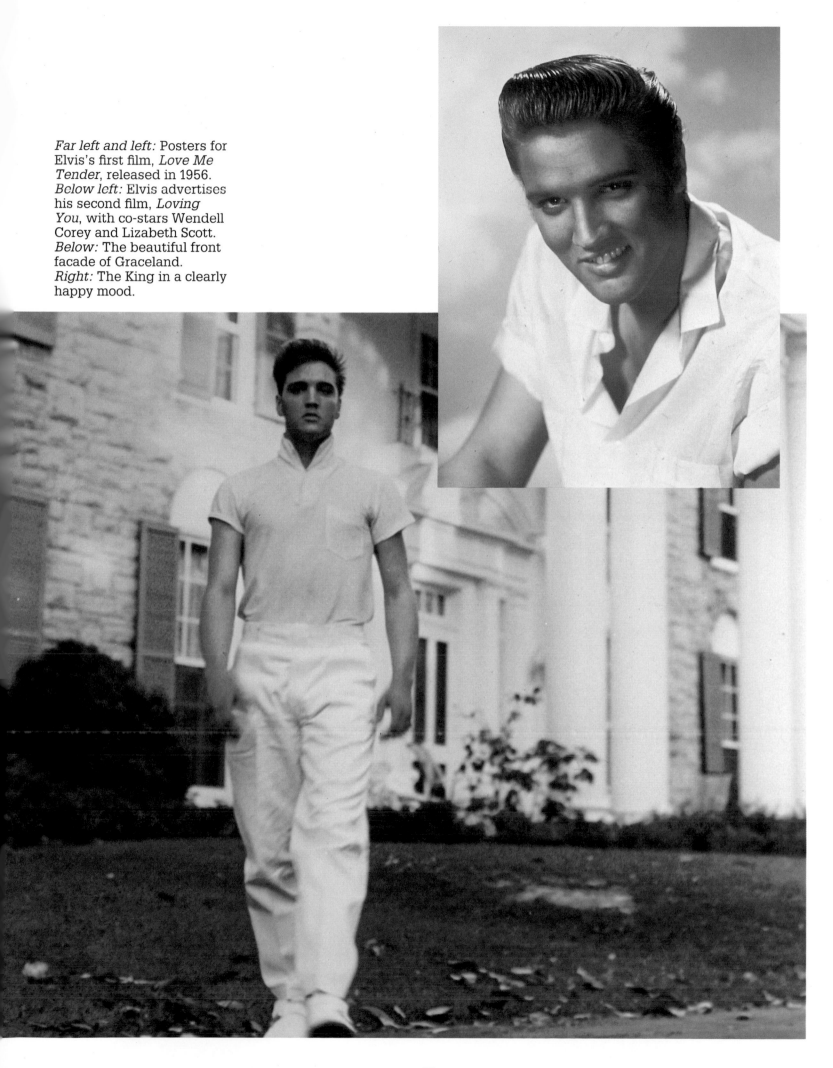

Far left and left: Posters for Elvis's first film, *Love Me Tender*, released in 1956.
Below left: Elvis advertises his second film, *Loving You*, with co-stars Wendell Corey and Lizabeth Scott.
Below: The beautiful front facade of Graceland.
Right: The King in a clearly happy mood.

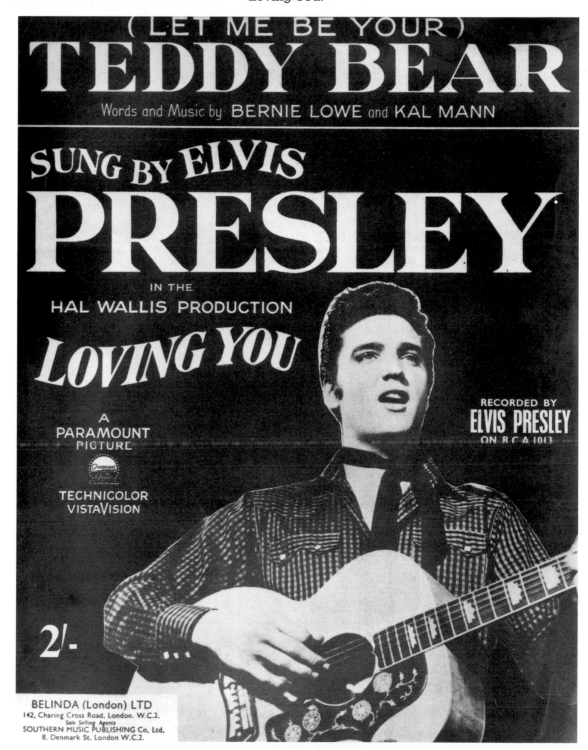
Far left: Elvis is watched over as he reads a note from . . . an admirer?
Left: The selling of the King – London-based magazine Picture Show offers its reader the shirt worn by Elvis in the film *Jailhouse Rock* and 50 signed photos.
Below left: A student contemplates taking a bite out of an Elvis Presley 'Teddy Bear' candy bar, while Elvis looks on.
Below: An advert for '(Let me be your) Teddy Bear,' one of Elvis's greatest hit taken from the film *Loving You.*

Left: Elvis performs in front of an audience in his hometown of Tupelo, Mississippi, 27 September 1956. The proceeds were donated to the town.
Below left and below: Scenes of teenage hysteria as Elvis rocks in front of an ecstatic crowd in Philadelphia, Pennsylvania.
Right: The fans go wild as Elvis belts out a song during the Tupelo concert.

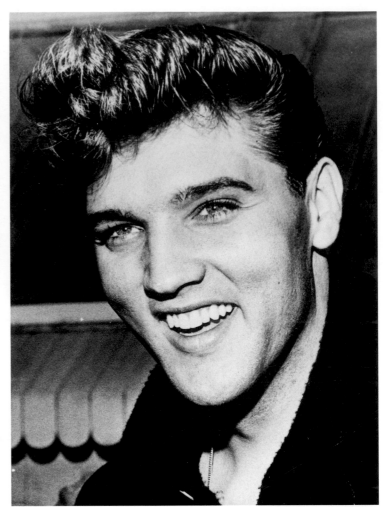

Above, far left: Elvis with two lucky fans.
Above left: Elvis celebrates his first No. 1 in the Country Charts – 'Mystery Train' – in 1955.
Far left: Takin' it easy!
Left: The King rocks at an open air show.
Above: Elvis makes his Las Vegas debut. His outrageous antics shocked the staid middle-aged audience.

Above & left: Elvis and the 'Blue Moon Boys' in 1955. They gave him loyal support during the early days, but resigned in the summer of 1957 because they didn't receive a fair share of Elvis's success. *Right:* Elvis became expert at karate and enjoyed showing off his prowess.

Elvis toured Florida in 1956 with a series of one-night stands that were the beginning of Elvis mania. He analyzed his act modestly, but fairly accurately: 'I'm not kiddin' myself. My voice alone is just an ordinary voice. What people come to see is how I use it. If I stand still when I'm singin' I'm a dead man. I might as well go back to driving a truck.'

Right & below: Elvis produced an energetic act. A doctor told him that he used as much energy in a 30 minute performance as a manual laborer in an eight-hour day.

Left & far left: As Col. Parker said, 'The kids are the ones that made Elvis . . .'

Below: 'I don't want him on my show, I don't care what anyone says about him or how great a talent he is'; this was Ed Sullivan's reaction to the rather dubious reputation of Elvis in 1956. Presley's appearance, however, produced record-breaking audience figures.

Elvis goes to Hollywood. Believing that his future success lay in movies, Elvis was delighted when producer Hal Wallis (*below left*) signed him for several films. Vernon and Gladys (*below right*) traveled to California to take care of 'their boy', and to watch him conquer Hollywood. *Right:* With Richard Egan in *Love Me Tender*, Elvis's first movie.

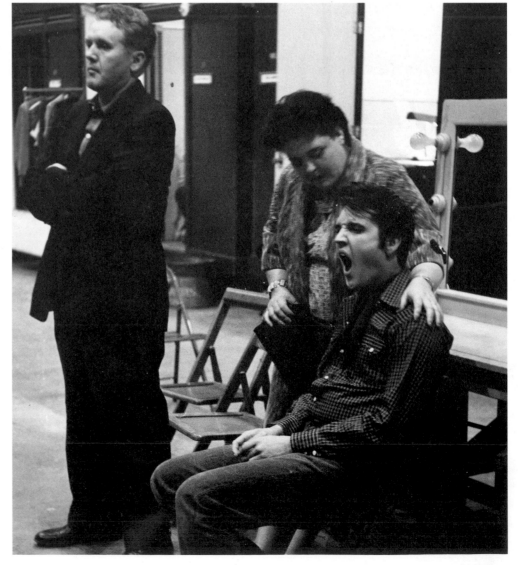

Elvis was billed after the stars Richard Egan and Debra Paget in his first movie, *Love Me Tender*, but it soon became clear who was the main attraction. Elvis gave one of his best performances as Clint Reno, although the director made the mistake of killing him off at the end. This provoked audience protests, so a ghostly Elvis was added to the final frames, singing the theme song.

Set during the Civil War, *Love Me Tender* was the story of two brothers who fell for the same girl. This naturally produced a certain amount of fraternal disagreement.

This page: Elvis became extremely fond of Debra Paget, his leading lady in *Love Me Tender*. She resisted his charm, despite a proposal of marriage.
Far right: Love Me Tender opened in New York on 15 November 1956 to mixed critical reviews, but rapturous audience receptions.

Left: Elvis with Barbara Lange in Hollywood, February 1957.
Right: One of the first singers to wear make-up on stage, Elvis really didn't mind being submitted to the make-up artist before film or TV work.

Elvis began work on his second movie, *Loving You*, in early 1957. The film was released in July while he was on a concert tour.

Elvis played Deke Rivers, a poor country boy who joined a traveling hillbilly band and sang his way to success. Backed by 'The Jordannaires', his usual band, *Loving You* included rock'n'roll classics like 'Let's Have a Party,' 'Hot Dog,' and 'Got a Lot of Living to do.'

Elvis's co-stars in *Loving You* were Lizabeth Scott, who played Glenda the ambitious publicist, and Dolores Hart, who appeared as Deke's girlfriend.

Left & below: Elvis at Paramount Studios during the filming of *Loving You*. *Right:* Elvis himself was unattainable, but some lucky fans captured the next best thing – a lifesize cutout of the King used to advertise *Loving You*.

Surrounded by the trappings of a Hollywood star. *Above*, with Miss Texas, 1957.
Below: A bizarre picture of Elvis, the Colonel (second right), and various movie moghuls. The significance of the goatee beards remains a mystery.
Right: 'He was so square he was fascinating'. Natalie Wood's verdict on a date with Elvis.

Jailhouse Rock was Elvis's third movie in less than a year. By now well accustomed to Hollywood ways, he began work on it in May 1957. He was committed to a grueling schedule, but still found time for relaxation and promotional stunts (*far left and right*).

Elvis played Vince Everett, a self-centered tough guy who learns to play the guitar in jail. *Jailhouse Rock* was an instant hit, and is now a rock'n'roll classic.

Left: Elvis choreographed the spectacular song-and-dance sequence that is so famous, and for once the blurb on the poster (*top right*) was no exaggeration. *Below right:* At MGM studios, 1957.

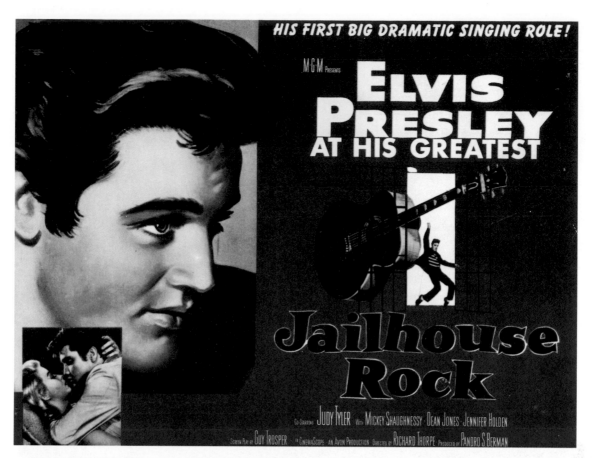

HIS FIRST BIG DRAMATIC SINGING ROLE!

M·G·M PRESENTS

ELVIS PRESLEY AT HIS GREATEST

Jailhouse Rock

Co-Starring JUDY TYLER · With MICKEY SHAUGHNESSY · DEAN JONES · JENNIFER HOLDEN

Screen Play by GUY TROSPER · IN CinemaScope · AN AVON PRODUCTION · Directed by RICHARD THORPE · Produced by PANDRO S BERMAN

By Christmas 1957, Elvis's new-found wealth and fame had made a huge difference to his family's lifestyle, and his parents basked in their son's reflected glory. Earlier in the year he had purchased Graceland, the mansion where he could cut himself off from the world and live as he pleased.

3 GI BLUES?

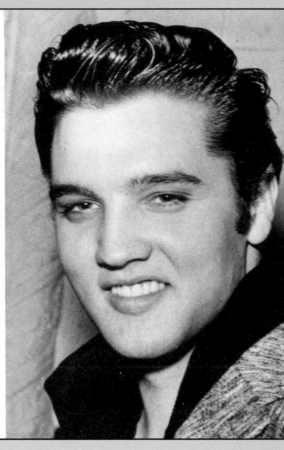

24 March 1958 – the day
Elvis Presley, the King of
rock'n'roll left home, lost
his sideburns and quiff,
and became US53310761.

Elvis's induction into the army at Fort Chafee was one of the most photographed events of the year. Colonel Parker had arranged a media circus for a willing press who recorded all but the most intimate moments of what should have been routine administration. The Colonel realized that this would probably be the rock King's last appearance for two years, and he wanted to give the fans something to drool over. Even Elvis, who was never usually shy of a photo-opportunity, became annoyed by the Colonel's continual interference and, aware that he was about to lose the most famous sideburns and quiff in the world, felt particularly humiliated by his trip to the army barber.

After a few days at Fort Chaffee, Elvis was sent to Fort Hood, Texas, for training as a tanker. Despite the fact the half the men in his platoon collapsed, Elvis survived basic training and actually emerged as a good soldier. He was due to be posted to Germany in September 1957, a fact which upset his mother, despite his constant reassurances that she would come too. As the date of Elvis's departure loomed nearer, Gladys became gradually more incapacitated with jaundice. Elvis was devoted to his mother and her death in August 1957 devastated him.

Having given a long press conference before he left the US which was later released as an EP, 'Elvis Sails,' he arrived in Germany to the familiar sound of screaming teenagers. Once installed at Bad Neuheim, the Presley family and retainers arrived. Elvis claimed his father and grandmother as dependents and lived with them off-base in a rented house, 14 Goethestrasse. The presence of his family made the unfamiliar surroundings more comfortable for Elvis, but nothing could disguise the fact that army life was completely alien to him. For a start, he had to get up at 4.30 am, the time he normally stopped partying. Once he arrived on base he behaved and was treated just like any other soldier, but at home he lived, as far as possible, a rock star's life. He was chauffered to work in the 'Elviswagen' and employed several assistants to deal with the vast quantity of fan mail that arrived every day. Unlike his comrades in arms, he really lived the life of a recluse, simply because he was mobbed every time he tried to visit a local bar or cinema. Despite the sign outside his house stating that autographs would be signed only between 7.30 and 8.00 pm each day, a posse of fans was permanently stationed there.

Elvis was employed by the army in a reconnais-

sance unit and spent most of his time familiarizing himself with the countryside, or surveying the border. Had the Soviets ever invaded it would have been Elvis's unit that led the tanks into battle. It was generally cold, boring work, but Elvis acquitted himself well, and had earned his sergeant's stripes by the time he was discharged. The military authorities were pleased with him: 'This guy Elvis has made It popular to be a good soldier. It's great for us.'

It was while he was in Germany that he met Priscilla Beaulieu, the girl who later became his wife. Elvis surrounded himself with young people in his off-duty hours, and enjoyed old-fashioned family entertainment around the piano — a far cry from the frenetic lifestyle of 'Elvis the Pelvis.' Introduced to Priscilla by an army colleague, Elvis was immediately attracted to her, partly because she was so pretty, and partly because he was lonely and met few American girls. He went out of his way to impress her, singing and playing the piano. Priscilla was overwhelmed: she was only 14 years old, yet she was alone with the greatest teen-idol in the world. She looked considerably older than her years, and appears to have been extremely self-possessed. Elvis spent hours alone with her, pour-

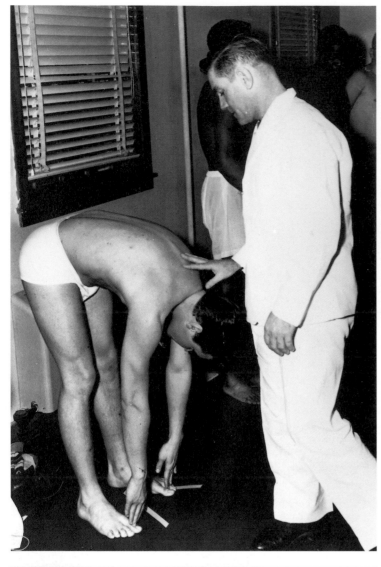

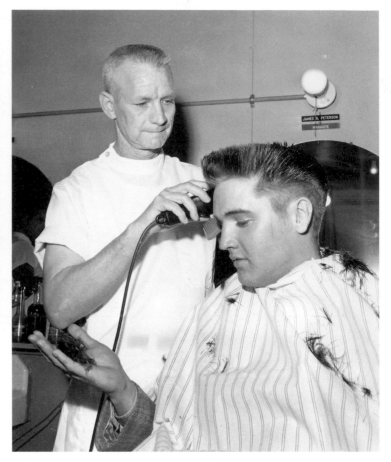

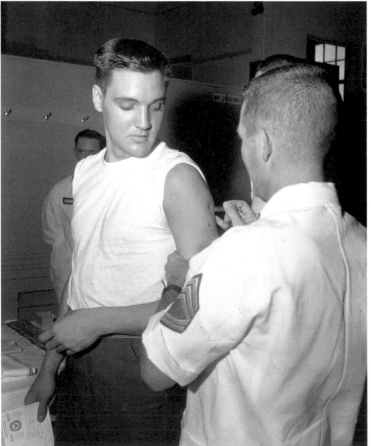

ing out his troubles. Unlike other girls she seemed concerned about him for himself, rather than his status as the most famous man in the Western hemisphere. Her parents were at first perturbed by Priscilla's nocturnal visits to Elvis's home, but relaxed slightly after meeting him, when he won them over with his Southern charm and honesty. Priscilla remained a fairly well-kept secret – Elvis didn't want a reputation like Jerry Lee Lewis who had just been universally denounced for marrying his 13-year-old cousin. One photographer, however, was aware of the secret, and his pictures of Priscilla waving goodbye to Elvis as he left for America have a haunting quality.

Elvis left the army in a similar manner to which he joined – in a blaze of publicity. He arrived to a vast welcome home reception orchestrated by Colonel Parker and attended by droves of press photographers. Much to everyone's relief, the public had not forgotten Elvis and the way seemed clear for him to pick up his career where he had left off.

The world's press participated in almost every aspect of Elvis's army induction – *Life* magazine alone filed 1,200 pictures. Elvis seemed slightly embarrassed by all the attention, only managing a sheepish quip, 'Hair today gone tomorrow.'

When his mother became ill in August 1958 Elvis obtained emergency leave and kept a 36-hour vigil at her bedside with his father. When she died of a heartattack, Elvis was completely inconsolable.

When Elvis was posted to Germany in September 1958, he gave a long press conference at the quayside, announcing 'I'm looking forward to my first furlough in Paris, I'd like to meet Brigitte Bardot.' He marched up the gangplank to the sound of a marine band playing, rather incongruously, a medley of his hits.

Above, below and far right:
The strumming G.I. with
Bill Haley, who toured
Europe in 1959.

Right: Elvis on leave in
Paris. 'I loved Paris. I didn't
have to sign many
autographs and became an
ordinary guy for a while.'

The Army offered Elvis the chance to 'do a Glenn Miller' and join the Special Services where he would have spent his time entertaining troops. Col. Parker advised him to join a regular unit, then no-one could accuse Elvis of opting out, or the Army of favoritism. In fact Elvis's military career gave both him and the Army a lot of favorable publicity.

Elvis was posted to a combat-ready armored division stationed in Friedburg. A colleague said of him, 'He sat on his butt in the snow like the rest of us, and ate the same crummy food we did. He was a real Joe.'

The last film Elvis made before his call-up was *King Creole*: his draft date was deferred by 60 days so that he could complete filming.

King Creole gave Elvis his first serious dramatic role, and is generally regarded as his most successful performance as an actor. he is pictured (*far right*) with producer Hal Wallis, and (*above*) with Dolores Hart.

Based on the Harold Robbins novel, *A Stone for Danny Fisher*, Elvis played Danny, a young nightclub singer who becomes involved with gangsters. Set in New Orleans, *King Creole* easily captures the captivating, sleazy mood of the city.

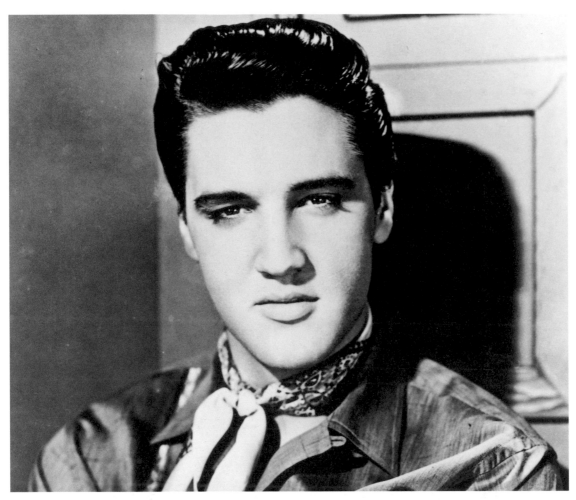

As Danny, Elvis was drawn to two women, Ronnie his girlfriend, and Maxie, the nightclub owner (both pictured right kissing Elvis).

Elvis flew home from Germany on 2 March 1960. He hated flying, but the 14-hour flight was broken only by a refueling stop at Prestwick, Scotland. The DC-7 landed at McGuire Field near Fort Dix, New Jersey in a blizzard, bringing the King safely home.

Priscilla Beaulieu stands out from the crowd at Frankfurt airport as she waves goodbye to Elvis. Reporters quickly discovered that she was 'the girl he left behind' and arranged a photo session. For a 14-year-old girl the sudden publicity must have been alarming, but Priscilla seems to have taken it all in her stride.

Despite the appalling weather, a huge crowd turned out to welcome Elvis, and he seemed to enjoy the carnival atmosphere as much as anyone.

Colonel Parker organized a mammoth press conference for Elvis's arrival, which included a personal welcome from Nancy Sinatra. Reporters gleefully conveyed this news to a dismayed Priscilla thousands of miles away in Germany.

4 HOLLYWOOD

Almost as soon as Elvis emerged from the army it became clear that his professional image had radically altered. The confident sneer and wild gyrations had been replaced by a clean-cut, wholesome Elvis; the dangerous 'Pelvis' had disappeared forever. Colonel Parker had never been entirely happy with Elvis's rebellious image, and evidently believed that his long-term career prospects could only be improved by making him acceptable to 'middle America'. The fire of Elvis's music was damped down and, arguably, never burnt as strongly again. Elvis went to Hollywood to pursue his dream of movie stardom, and was not given the opportunity to perform live for nearly ten years.

With retrospect, this decision seems misguided, even criminal. In 1960 the world of rock'n'roll was in a parlous state, its heroes crushed or dead: Buddy Holly and Ritchie Valens were gone, Gene Vincent paralyzed, and the career of Jerry Lee Lewis blighted by scandal. The return of the King seemed like a godsend to the fans.

In April 1960 Elvis was closeted in a Nashville recording studio for 24 hours and the songs he produced were indicative of the new direction of his career. There was nothing to set the kids' blue suede shoes jiving; instead the two best-selling tunes were powerful ballads, 'Are You Lonesome Tonight?' and 'It's Now or Never.' The Colonel's next move was to arrange for Elvis to appear on the slightly bizarre TV special, *Frank Sinatra's Welcome Home Party for Elvis*, for which Elvis received the unprecedented fee of $125,000. It marked a new alliance between Elvis and the crooners of the '50s who had originally viewed the young star with suspicion, if not outright hostility.

For an immensely successful singer to abandon the career that made him famous may seem foolhardy, but both Elvis and the Colonel were convinced that his future was in movies. And indeed, the Colonel had arranged what appeared to be a lucrative multi-movie deal whereby Elvis would make three pictures a year for nine years. The main

Elvis in various guises during the 1960s. *Left*, as Ross Carpenter in *Girls, Girls, Girls; above*, as pilot Mike Edwards in *It Happened at the World's Fair; right*, as Tulsa Maclean in *GI Blues*.

122

problem was that this arrangement did not encourage the production of quality films. From 1961 Elvis starred in successive sun'n'fun movies, all with similar halting plots involving Elvis, a gaggle of girls, and an album's worth of songs. Some, such as *Blue Hawaii*, did enormously well at the box office. Others, such as *Follow That Dream* were instantly forgettable, unwatched by even the most ardent fans. It was a scheme designed to make a lot of money with very little effort. It was also a chronic waste of Elvis's potential.

The first few films of the '60s were probably the best of the bunch. *G I Blues* cashed in on Elvis's recent military experience. He miserably agreed to retain his regulation haircut and dug out his khaki fatigues for his role as Tulsa Maclean, a GI stationed in Frankfurt who becomes involved with a local girl. The rebellious, menacing James Dean-manqué of *Jailhouse Rock* was gone, replaced by a

benign, patriotic fellow who performed numbers with puppets, backed by a children's chorus. If the fans were shocked by this change, their hero was also distinctly underwhelmed by the movie and demanded that he be given a serious dramatic role with no singing.

Flaming Star (1960) was a psychological western about a half-breed Indian torn between two cultures; the leading role had originally been offered to Brando, and the director was Don Siegel who had made *Invasion of the Body Snatchers*. Movies did not come much more 'serious', and Elvis

Elvis's movie roles provided him with a lexicon of different careers – pilot, soldier, actor, bodyguard and acrobat. In this way, at least, he wasn't typecast.

accepted the part with alacrity. That the movie was not a roaring success was not the fault of its star. Elvis performed well, but the action tended to flag; the fans would really have preferred a cheerful musical, but the critics were mildly impressed. 'Despite familiar absurdities it has more than its share of good moments,' wrote one, but the box office receipts did not match even such muted praise. Elvis's next movie, *Wild in the Country*, achieved neither fame nor fortune, and marked the end of his foray into 'serious' acting. From now on it was downhill all the way, with a series of vapid vehicles that were lucrative, but essentially unsatisfying for their star.

Many fans have wondered why Elvis continued to associate himself with such films. It is clear that he was depressed by their quality and he complained frequently to the Colonel. It is unfortunate that his only attempts at serious roles had been box-office disasters, because in the Colonel's eyes, financial success was the only worthwhile yardstick with which to judge a movie. Elvis was apparently the highest paid actor in Hollywood and reaped 50 percent of the profits from each film. He had grown accustomed to a lavish lifestyle and really had no choice but to work according to the contracts his manager had negotiated.

The depressing ritual of churning out three movies a year affected Elvis both personally and professionally. While he was making 'B' movies the music industry had found new heroes whose popularity rivaled that of Elvis. Dylan, the Beatles, and the Rolling Stones received the same kind of hysterical adulation once accorded Elvis: there were now pretenders to his throne. Elvis was not the only singer to make movies, but when compared to *A Hard Day's Night*, or *Sergeant Pepper*, the Presley movies seem like dated relics of an old Hollywood.

By 1969 Elvis had been isolated from mainstream rock culture for most of the decade. He released 'Suspicious Minds' in the same year as Woodstock and his music seemed a million miles away from the outpourings of Hendrix, the Grateful Dead or Janis Joplin. The question hanging over his career at the end of the decade was whether the once-great King of rock'n'roll had had his day.

It Happened at the World's Fair projected the mature, responsible Elvis, who could fly, babysit *and* sing.

Elvis slipped easily into most roles, be they diver, racing driver or singer. At the base of each character was a talented musician, which is obviously what appealed most to him.

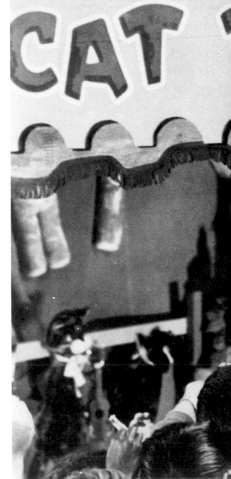

Far left: Double Trouble.
Top: Clambake
Left: Roustabout
Above: A favorite image –
Elvis protecting a
distressed female in
Flaming Star.

131

Released in 1963, *Fun in Acapulco* paired Elvis with Ursula Andress, who was still fresh from her success as the first 'Bond girl' in *Dr No*.

Easy Come, Easy Go touched briefly on avant-garde body painting – definitely a first in one of Elvis's movies.
Right & far right: Harum Scarum and *Frankie and Johnnie* presented more familiar pleasures, while *Double Trouble (top right)* let Elvis do what he was best at.

Far left: As Pacer Burton in *Flaming Star*.
This page: The bevy of beauties who surrounded Elvis in this film ensured that it lived up to its title – *Girls, Girls, Girls*.

Racing driver, tortured cowboy, boxer, and an acrobat with vertigo – stills from *Spinout, Charro, Kid Galahad* and *Fun in Acapulco*.

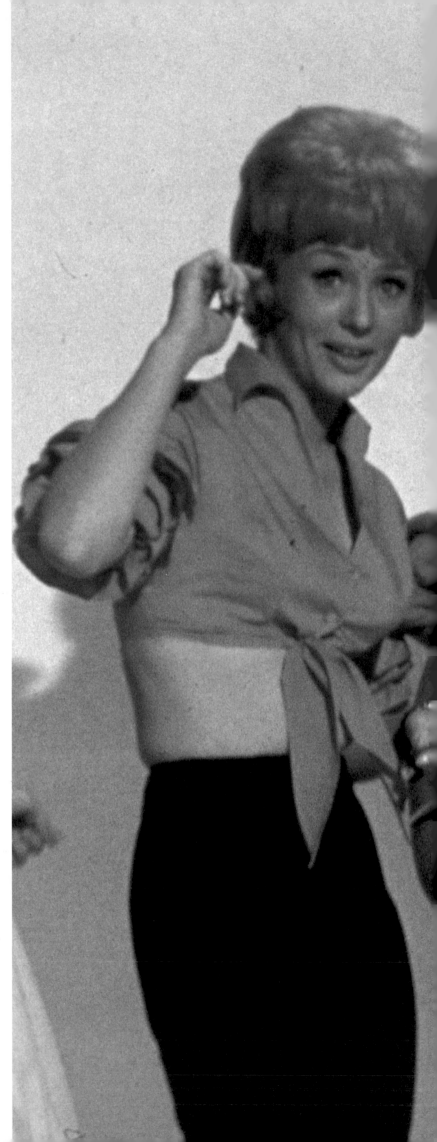

There is evidence that Elvis was not entirely happy with the direction of his film career in the mid-1960s, but he seems to be coping in these stills.

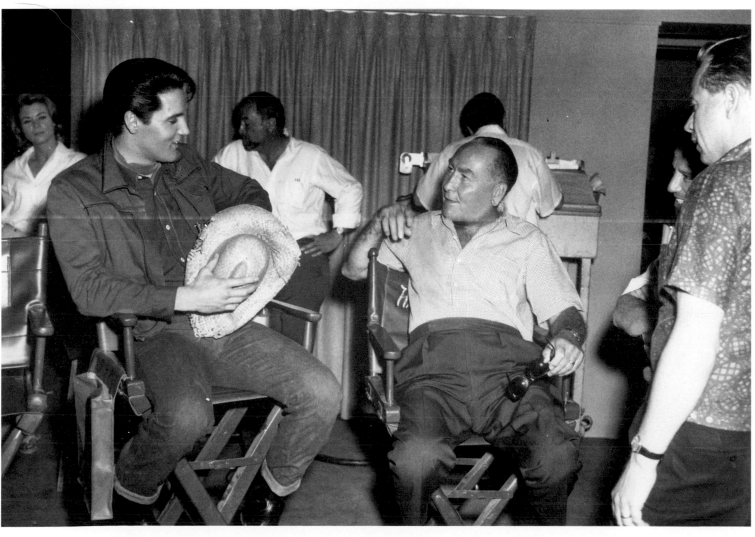

Far left: Released in 1962, *It Happened at the World's Fair* cast Elvis as pilot Mike Edwards whose love life was complicated by the presence of a 7-year-old orphan.
Left: An increasingly familiar pose that occurred in most of his movies.
Below: Elvis chats with producer Hal Wallis on the set of *Roustabout*.

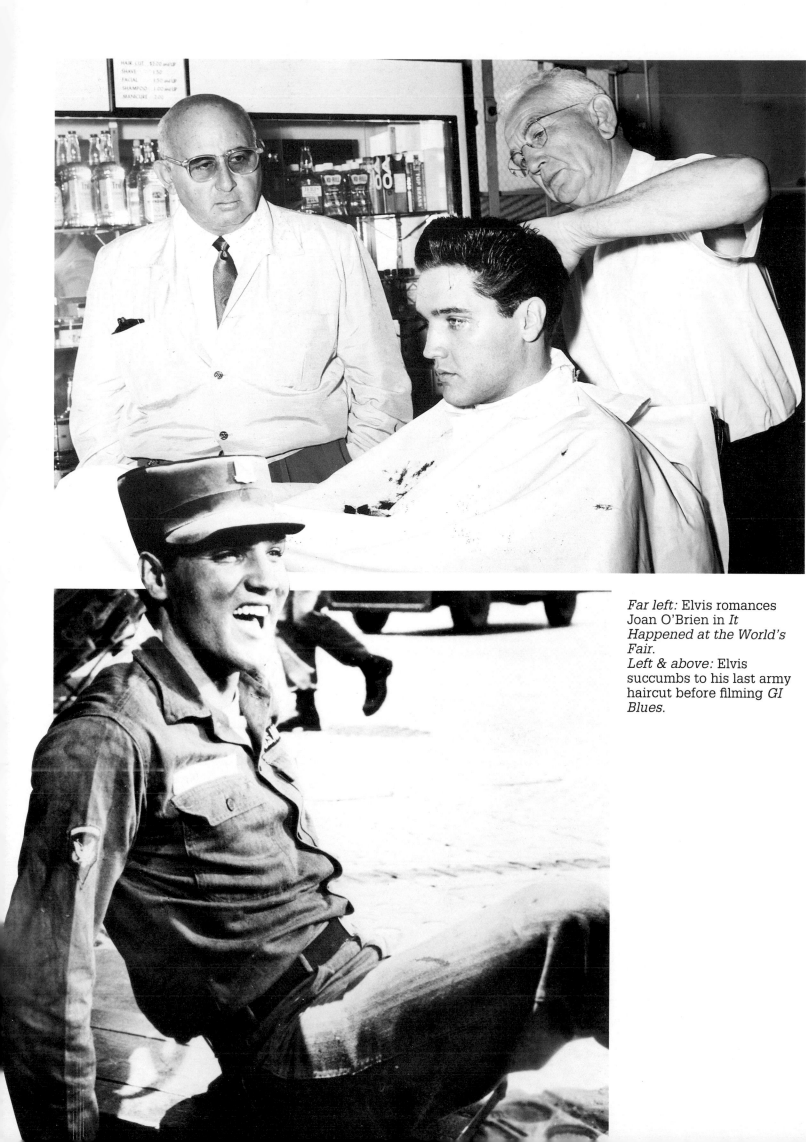

Far left: Elvis romances Joan O'Brien in *It Happened at the World's Fair.*
Left & above: Elvis succumbs to his last army haircut before filming *GI Blues.*

GI Blues, Elvis's first film after his release from the Army was partly autobiographical. Elvis played Tulsa Maclean, a GI stationed in Germany, who becomes involved with Lili, a cabaret singer (Juliet Prowse). This movie provided the hit single 'Wooden Heart.'

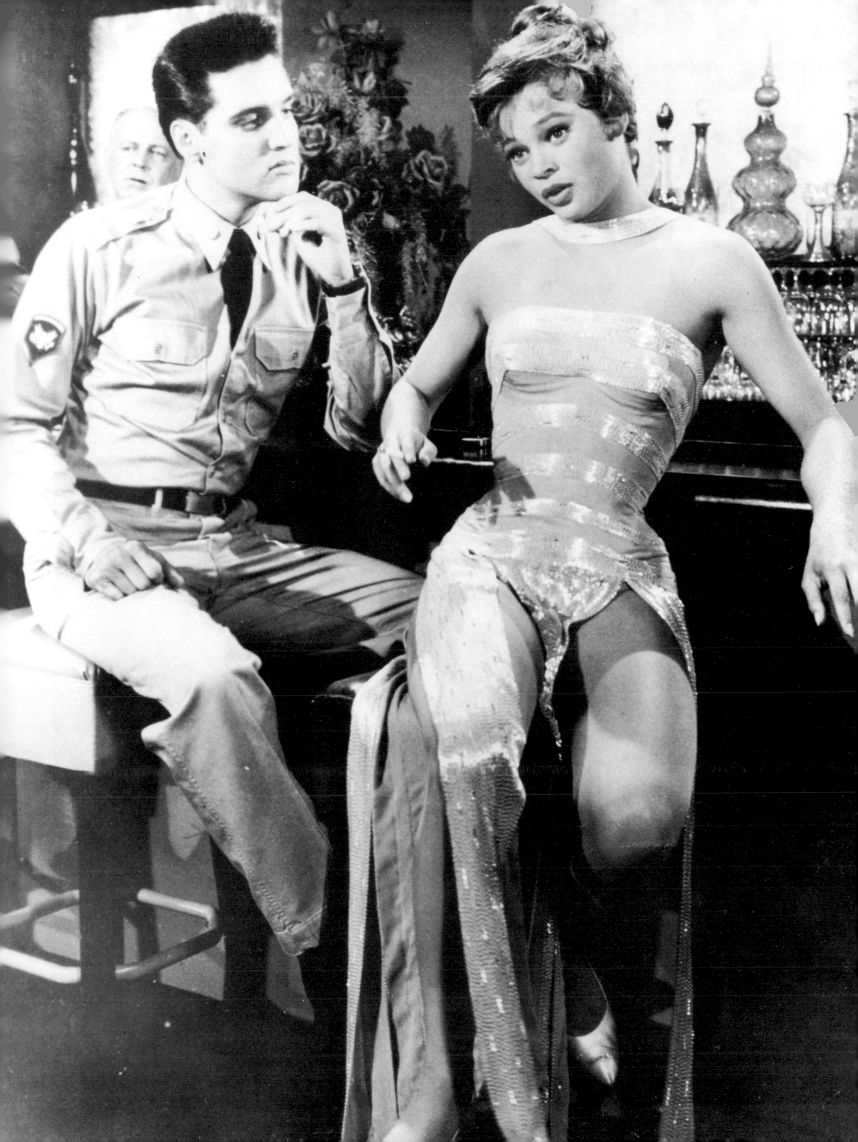

GI Blues (above) was swiftly followed by *Flaming Star*, a psychological western in which Elvis starred with Steve Forrest and Barbara Eden. Elvis delivered a fine performance as Pacer Burton, the half-breed Indian torn between two cultures, but this 'serious' movie did not appeal to most of his fans.

Like *Flaming Star (right and below)*, *Wild in the Country* was poorly received, although Elvis had an interesting role as the sexy, southern youth Glen Tyler. He is pictured *far right* with Millie Perkins, *center* with Tuesday Weld, and *below far right* with Hope Lange.

Perhaps overcome by their celluloid characters in *Wild in the Country*, Tuesday Weld was moved to remark 'Elvis is the nicest guy ever. I think I'd like to marry him.'

In *Blue Hawaii* Elvis makes another appearance as a GI newly released from the Army. The son of a pineapple tycoon, he returns home to his girlfriend, Joan Blackman and realizes that he doesn't want to enter the family business. It was an immensely successful movie, grossing $4.7 million, which must have pleased producer Hal Wallis (*above*).

Follow that Dream (1962), was a romantic comedy in which Elvis's wandering family tried to set up home on a Florida beach – which provoked a predictable reaction from the authorities.

156

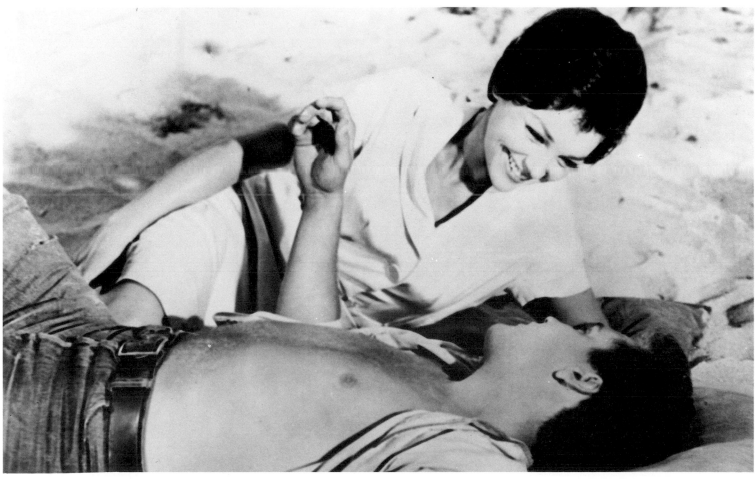

A musical remake of the 1937 film, *Kid Galahad* presented Elvis as Walter Gulick, a poor sparring partner who punches his way to fame. Released in 1962, *Kid Galahad* was slightly different from his other films, in that for once, Elvis played a character who knew what he wanted from life.

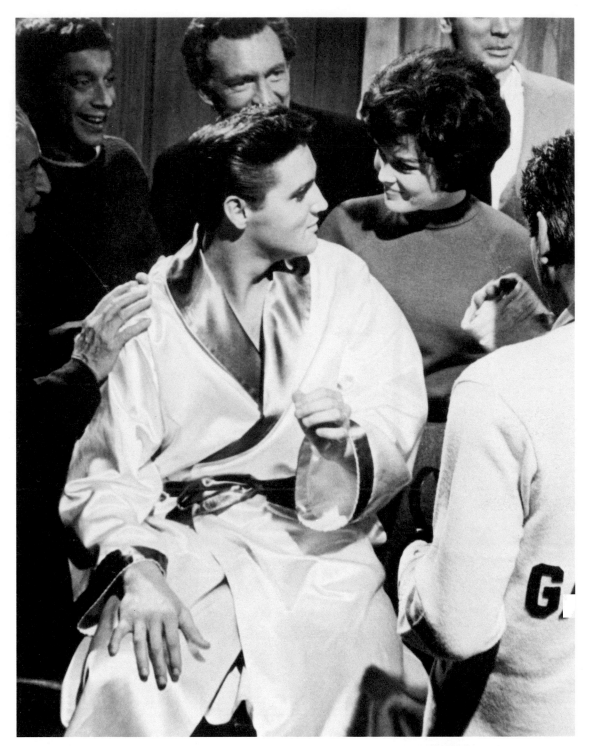

Appearing with Elvis in
Girls, Girls, Girls were
Stella Stevens, Laurel
Goodwin (*far right*) and
Jeremy Slate.

Girls, Girls, Girls, was a light musical romance that featured the hit song 'Return to Sender'.

The hero of *Girls, Girls, Girls,* was Ross Carpenter, a nightclub singer trying to return to the family trade of fishing.

Elvis lands in touble with
co-star Gary Lockwood in *It
Happened at the World's
Fair*. By the end of the film
the playboy pilot is a
reformed character.

More stills from the 1962 hit *Girls, Girls, Girls*. If Elvis appears a little detached it may be because he had just been reunited with Priscilla after a two year absence.

Playing a responsible guardian was a new role for Elvis, but he carried it off successfully in *It Happened at the World's Fair*.

As the wayward son of Angela Lansbury (*left*), Elvis abandoned the parental home to become a guide and beachcomber to a party of pretty young college girls in *Blue Hawaii*. *Right:* The beachcomber becomes a pilot – Elvis in *It Happened at the World's Fair*.

Released in 1963, *Fun in Acapulco* starred Elvis as Mike Wingren, a trapeeze artist who becomes afraid of heights. He takes up a job as a lifeguard, which doesn't seem to be any safer . . .

Released in December 1966, *Spinout* had Elvis as Mike McCoy, racing driver and leader of a rock band.

Far right: Elvis prepares for a scene in *Fun in Acapulco*, (Paramount, November 1963).

Main picture: Elvis and Barbara Stanwyck, the stars of *Roustabout*. Elvis's character, Charlie Rogers, is discovered to have a great singing voice.
Left and below left: Two stills from *Kissin' Cousins* in which Elvis has two roles, rivals Josh Morgan and Jodie Tatum.
Right: Roustabout was released by Paramount in November 1964. Here Elvis flirts with one of the chorus line.

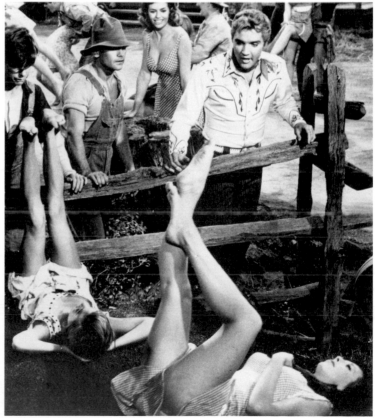

These pages: A selection of dramatic scenes from *Kissin' Cousins*, including (*far left*) a confrontation between two Presleys!

These pages: Elvis at work, rest and play in *Viva Las Vegas.* Elvis starred with the beautiful actress Ann-Margret (*above top, far right* and *above, far right*) in this MGM movie released in 1964.

These pages: Paradise Hawaiian Style, saw Elvis playing a helicopter pilot who shows vacationers the beauties of the islands.

Above: Elvis has a run-in
with the law during *Viva
Las Vegas*. Remarkably, the
film was released a little
more than a month after
Kissin' Cousins.
Right and far right: Elvis in
action during *Roustabout* –
dealing with the low sheriff
and a troublemaker at the
carnival where he worked.

These pages: Easy Come Easy Go saw Elvis play navy demolitions man Ted Jackson and the plot revolves around the legend of a lost treasure hidden in a sunken wreck off the coast of California. The film co-starred Dodie Marshall, whose character was won by Elvis.

These pages: Roustabout had Elvis teamed up with two Hollywood greats – Barbara Stanwyck and Jack Albertson. Stanwyck gives Elvis his big singing break, allowing him to perform at her carnival. Songs in the film included 'One Track Mind,' 'I Never Had It So Good,' and 'Hard Knocks.'

These pages: Girl Happy was released in 1965 and had Elvis playing a bodyguard who was on hand to protect the daughter of a Chicago nightclub owner from the amorous advances of beach-bums in Fort Lauderdale, Florida. Elvis sang his way through 'Puppet on a String' and 'Do the Clam.'

These pages: Elvis played the role of Lonnie Beale in *Tickle Me* (1964), a radio writer who takes on a job at a beauty farm. He performs 'Dirty, Dirty Feelings,' 'It's a Long, Lonely Highway,' and 'It Feels so Right' in the film.

Elvis was enthusiastic about *Harum Scarum* (1965) because he thought the role of Johnnie Tyrone was similar to that played by his hero Rudolph Valentino in *The Sheikh*.

Paradise Hawaiian Style released by Paramount in 1966, was a natural successor to the box-office hit *Blue Hawaii*.

Released as *California Holiday* in Britain, *Spinout* was a film in which Elvis got to drive fast cars – a favorite hobby.

As a singing racing driver, Elvis was pursued by virtually every female who appeared in *Spinout*.

Elvis appeared as Scott Heyward in *Clambake*, a millionaire's son who swaps identities with a waterskiing instructor.

This page and overleaf: Double Trouble was filmed in 1967, featuring Elvis as Guy Lambert, a singer mistakenly pursued as a jewel thief. Elvis said of his role: 'I wasn't exactly James Bond . . . but no-one ever asked Sean Connery to sing a song while dodging bullets.'

Tickle Me showed Elvis in another energetic role, as an unemployed rodeo star. *Overleaf:* It became clear as the decade wore on that Elvis was the sole reason for the success of his movies. Regardless of content, fans flocked to see the King.

In 1965 Hollywood producer Hal Wallis said of Elvis: 'He was a national sensation on records, on TV, and in personal appearances when I signed him. But everybody told me I was crazy – he was just a flash in the pan. Now, ten years later, he's bigger than ever.

Elvis made three movies a
year for most of the '60s.
One director said of him
'He is the most co-operative
actor I ever met. He always
stopped for fans to give
autographs, even though I
knew he was worrying
about the next scene.'

5 THE KING IN HIS CASTLE

During the 1960s Elvis lived a peripatetic existence shuttling between Memphis and Hollywood. Although he owned a succession of homes on the West Coast he was happiest at Graceland, the one place he felt he could truly relax surrounded by his family and friends. Although it appeared that Elvis led a reclusive lifestlye, he was seldom alone; he was usually accompanied by an entourage of friends and relatives who acted not only as his roadies, accountants and PR men, but also as paid companions who could be summoned at any time of the day or night to amuse the King. They were known as the 'Memphis Mafia', a soubriquet Elvis encouraged in his later years by designing the famous 'Taking Care of Business' flash, and ensuring that the guys were equipped with his favorite law-enforcement badges procured from friendly sheriffs. The trailers and mobile homes of their families in the grounds of Graceland, gave the air of a traditional plantation.

Elvis was a generous employer, never hesitating to help out financially if one of the guys was in trouble. According to Priscilla Presley's account of life with Elvis, if he took up a hobby, he wanted everyone else to join in too. When Elvis discovered that he enjoyed riding, he purchased horses for the whole entourage, as well as their wives.

Elvis was really a nocturnal person, however, going to bed at four or five in the morning and rising at two in the afternoon. It was not unusual for him to spend evenings cruising around Memphis in one of his magnificent cars, or to hire a movie theater, or even a whole fairground. These may seem like the actions of a star who was ostentatious with his money, but with the most recognized face in the USA, a normal evening at the movies was just not feasible.

One of the more bizarre aspects of Elvis's private life was his relationship with Priscilla Beaulieu. In 1962, aged 16, Priscilla effectively moved in with Elvis, an event that could have provoked acres of damning newsprint had it become public knowledge. Although Elvis did not exactly flaunt Priscilla (she continued her schooling in Memphis while he was filming in Hollywood, for example), he didn't hide her either, frequently being seen in public with her. Priscilla's parents seemed content with the arrangements; Elvis had promised that Priscilla would lodge with his father, Vernon, and his wife, and would finish her education in Mem-

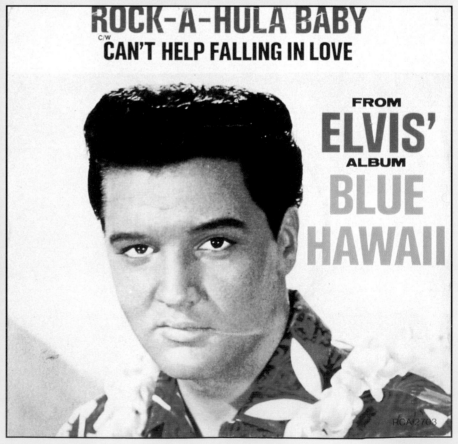

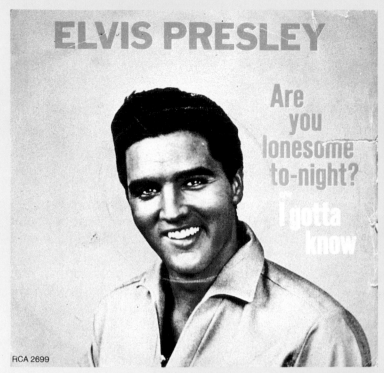

ELVIS PRESLEY

Are you lonesome to-night?

I gotta know

RCA 2699

ELVIS SINGS

RETURN TO SENDER

and

WHERE DO YOU COME FROM?

RCA 2706

Far left: Elvis was a keen collector of police badges, and this was the pride of his collection. Convinced that he could influence young people to kick their bad habits, Elvis persuaded President Nixon to make him a Federal Narcotics Agent in 1969.
Left & above: A selection of record covers from the 1960s.

Although Elvis acknowledged Priscilla as the serious love of his life, he flirted outrageously with many of his leading ladies and probably had affairs with a few of them. Fatuous quotations like Tuesday Weld's 'Elvis is the nicest guy ever, I think I'd like to marry him', were snapped up by the press, and rumors of his liaisons drifted back to Graceland and upset Priscilla dreadfully. By the end of the decade she learnt to ignore Elvis's peccadillos and even indulged in one or two herself.

According to many accounts the collapse of his marriage devastated Elvis. The fact that Priscilla left him for another man was a huge blow to his pride, one from which he never really recovered. After the birth of Lisa Marie in 1968, Elvis withdrew from Priscilla, and she, in her turn developed new interests. In 1973 they divorced agreeing to share custody of Lisa Marie and remaining on friendly terms. For Priscilla, life away from Elvis's weird nocturnal regime was a revelation, but Elvis's lifestyle didn't really change. He continued his punishing and ultimately fatal schedule of concerts and partying, supported by a constant diet of pills.

After two years out of circulation while in the army, Elvis was keen to discover whether his old magic could still pull in the fans. In May 1960 he appeared on a TV special, *Frank Sinatra's Welcome Home Party for Elvis Presley*, which reminded anyone who may have missed the all-pervasive publicity that the King was back.

phis. She was enrolled at a convent school, where it quickly became well known that she was Elvis's girlfriend.

Despite his promises to her parents, Priscilla spent most of her time with Elvis. Once he had her under his own roof he dictated exactly how she should dress, and turned her into a female version of himself. A young woman of great natural beauty, Elvis preferred Priscilla with a jet black beehive and heavy make up, and Priscilla naturally bowed to Elvis's every whim. Terrified that he would lose interest in her, she stayed up partying every night until three or four, struggled out of bed in time for school, and was usually home by the time Elvis got up in mid-afternoon. It was a strange and tiring lifestlye for anyone, particularly an impressionable teenager.

They were eventually married in 1967 in an orchestrated cloak-and-dagger ceremony that was the work of the ubiquitous Colonel Parker. Instead of sharing the occasion with friends and relatives, large numbers of the world's press were invited to witness the nuptials. Elvis and Priscilla seemed bewildered by the whole affair and reacted by staging a proper wedding reception for their friends a few weeks later at Graceland. The Colonel was conspicuous by his absence.

Despite the adoration of millions of women, and a more serious dalliance with Ann-Margret, (*above*),

Elvis was basically a one-woman man. Priscilla (*left*) was probably the love of his life.

231

After living together for years Elvis and Priscilla finally tied the knot on 1 May 1967 in Las Vegas. To avoid the presence of hordes of unhappy fans, Colonel Parker laid meticulous plans for the wedding of the world's most eligible star. Priscilla later wrote: 'I would have given anything for one moment alone with my husband. But we were immediately rushed out for a photo session.'

Left: The legacy of years of stunning recording – Elvis's trophy room at Graceland. Elvis has sold in excess of one billion records worldwide.
Right: Elvis shows off his new bride – and her 3½ carat ring.

Not known for his generosity with money, Elvis's father Vernon (right) was an excellent accountant and kept a tight rein on his son's finances. *Far right:* Exactly nine months after his wedding, Elvis's only child, Lisa Marie, was born on 1 February 1968.

The birth of his daughter confirmed Elvis's public image as a fine example to the nation's youth. It didn't stop him enjoying the trappings of his wealth, however.

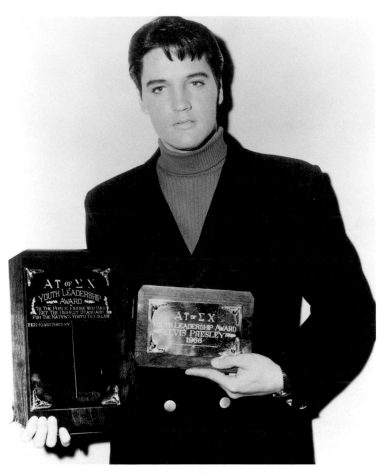

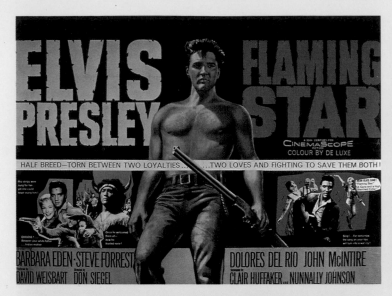

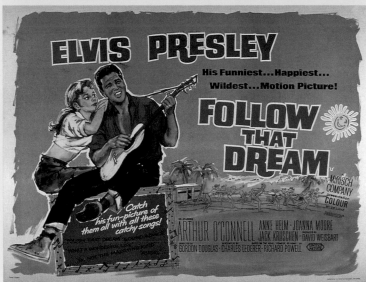

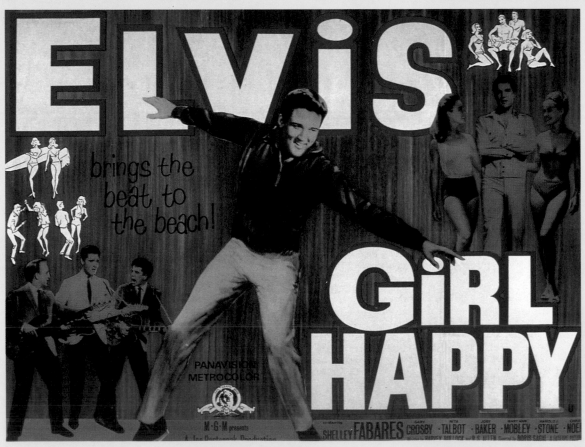

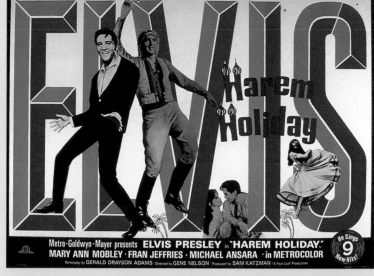

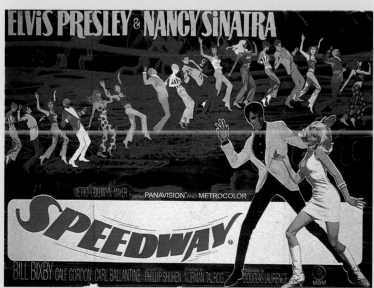

These pages: A selection of posters advertising just a few of Elvis's films. He completed over 30 pictures for a variety of studios between 1956 and 1969.

Above: Elvis and Nancy Sinatra during the filming of *Speedway*.
Above right: Issue 4 of the English fan magazine 'The Elvis Express.'

Below left: Elvis in his prime.
Below right: Elvis and Ann-Margret on the set of *Viva Las Vegas*.
Right: On location.

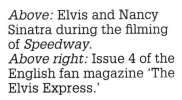

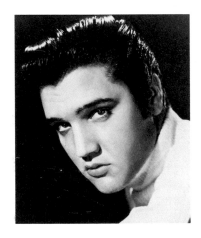

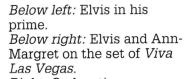

Above left: Elvis and his wife Priscilla arrive for an engagement. The couple met in 1959 and were wed in Las Vegas on 1 May 1967.
Far left: Elvis and Priscilla show their daughter, Lisa Marie, to the world. The baby daughter was born on 1 February 1968 at the Baptist Memorial Hospital in Memphis.
Left: Elvis in the studio.
Right: The King arrives for a show.

6 RESURGENCE

The musical career of Elvis Presley was salvaged by one man – Steve Binder – who worked against Colonel Parker's tacky demands to produce a spectacular TV special released for Christmas 1968 which captured Elvis at his best. He performed most of his hits from the fifties – but interestingly, not one song from his post-1960 movies. Clad in black leather, and as lean as he ever was, Elvis cut a dramatic figure. He seemed far more dangerous and interesting than the cuddly but dull characters of his recent movies. Elvis worked extremely hard on the project, far more enthusiastically than on any of his movies, and the resulting show was terrific. One rock critic wrote, '(it was) the finest music of his life', and this show reoriented Elvis. His movie career was little short of a joke; the reaction to the NBC show proved that not only was he a live performer to be taken seriously, but that this was where his future lay.

Elvis was motivated enough to return to the recording studio in Memphis and recorded so many numbers it took RCA over a year to release them. The King returned to the charts with new songs: 'In the Ghetto,' 'Kentucky Rain,' and 'Suspicious Minds.'

Having proved to himself and the world that he was still a dynamic live performer, Elvis was keen to hit the road and return to live concerts. He could have performed anywhere in the world – there was nothing to prevent him emulating Bob Dylan, for example, and appearing at a large open-air concert. Instead, the Colonel arranged a series of concerts in the newest and ritziest hotel in Las Vegas, the International. In many ways this was a strange choice of venue; it would surely have made more sense to present Elvis to a larger, younger audience than was the middle-aged norm in Vegas hotels. In addition the only time Elvis had performed there he had bombed, and he was not entirely happy about relaunching his musical career in the only US city to have booed him off the stage.

Aware of the potential pitfalls he planned his act carefully, eventually appearing on 26 July 1969 before a star-studded audience, and backed by a 30-piece orchestra. Before he could open his mouth he received a standing ovation, and from that moment, his confidence restored, Elvis enslaved the audience just as skilfully as when he was 22. It was the first time Priscilla had seen him perform live and she found him electrifying: 'At the end he left them still cheering and begging for more,' she wrote.

The next day, the International's manager, Alex Shoofey, lost no time in signing Elvis for two month-long appearances every year for five years on a salary of $1 million. Once again Elvis' professional life had been mapped out for him. He was

Left: Elvis in performance during 1968.
Right: A leather-clad Elvis belts out a number during his TV special, 3 December 1968.

These pages: Concert shots of Elvis taken in the second phase of his career in which he was renowned for his outrageous stage costumes.

tied to a long-term contract that in the long run was neither challenging nor particularly lucrative.

Having wowed Las Vegas, Elvis took his show on tour. He played 14 cities between 9 September and 17 November 1970, before returning to Vegas in January 1971 and then went on to Nashville for a long recording session. Life continued at this hectic pace throughout 1971 and 1972. In June his four days at Madison Square Garden set an all-time attendance record; a documentary of his concert performances, *Elvis on Tour*, won a Golden Globe award, and in January 1973 his *Aloha from Hawaii* show was broadcast to half a billion people in 40 countries. It really seemed as though the King was back in control.

During the first shows at least, Elvis was a spontaneous and dazzling performer who thrived on the adulation of the crowds. He designed stunning new stage suits, rehearsed hard and played to capacity audiences all over the US. However, he found it hard to come down to earth after each concert, and found that the only way to dissipate the adrenalin was to party through the remainder of the night. It was this kind of lifestyle that led to the deterioration of his health and appearance – the bloated face and ever-increasing girth. Committed to a punishing performance schedule, the novelty of performing live soon began to wear off and Elvis became tired. No one seemed to realize that he was no longer the energetic youngster who thrived on one-night stands; he was a man in early middle age and marginal health.

After his divorce from Priscilla in 1973 Elvis had two more serious relationships. The first was with Linda Thompson; Vernon believed that of all his women, she was the best for Elvis. She had the ability to match Elvis's moods and Elvis remained faithful to her for at least a year. 'He needed and wanted more love than anyone I've ever met. He was a super romantic.' Linda was completely devoted to him, but eventually the strain of pandering to every one of Elvis's bizarre whims became too much and they finally separated after three years in 1976.

Ginger Alden was another star-struck woman who caught Elvis's eye and who managed to captivate him. Nine weeks after meeting her he decided that they should be married and, on bended knee, he presented her with a huge diamond ring in his bathroom. Ginger was delighted: 'I felt that maybe that's why I was put on earth. If I could make Elvis happy, I would have served my purpose.'

Elvis's women may have made him happy, but neither they, nor anyone else close to him seemed able to prevent his dangerous intake of pills and drugs. A life-long insomniac, by the 1970s Elvis relied on a dangerous cocktail of prescription drugs to put him to sleep, wake him up and keep him going during the day. These accounted for his violent changes of mood and in the end, killed him.

Above, far left: Elvis lights Colonel Tom Parker's cigar. *Remaining pictures, these pages:* A selection of scenes from the 1968 MGM film *Stay Away Joe* which co-starred Burgess Meredith and Joan Blondell. Elvis plays a rough, tough character by the name of Joe Lightcloud.

'68 COMEBACK **SPECIAL**

These pages: A series of
photographs taken
throughout the King's
career showing him
performing live as well as
in the studio, and posing
for publicity shots.

Above and far right: Two stills from the film *Speedway*, a picture that proved something of a disappointment.
Right: Elvis in a clinch with an admirer during the making of *Stay Away Joe*.

Far left: Elvis and Nancy Sinatra dance the night away in *Speedway.*
Left; Nancy keeps the beat while the King belts out a song.
Below: Elvis and backing band performing in *Speedway.* Elvis played a racing car driver in the movie.

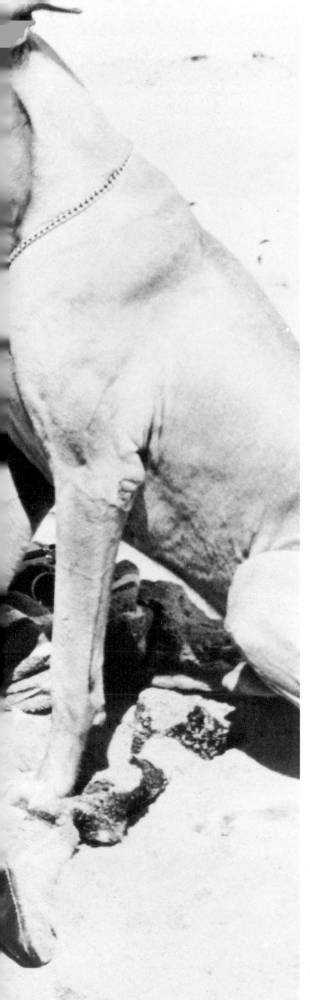

These pages: Live a Little, Love a Little was released by MGM in October 1968 and co-starred Michelle Carey (seen here). Elvis played the role of a fashion photographer.

264

Above: Elvis and Michelle Carey get to grips with each other in *Live a Little, Love a Little.*
Above left, far left and left: *Charro*, released by National General Productions Incorporated in September 1969, was the first and last picture that saw Elvis wear a beard.

These pages: Elvis playing Jess Wade in the film *Charro.* The only song on the film sound track occurred over the opening and closing credits.

These pages: Shots from *The Trouble with Girls*, a film released by MGM in December 1969. The movie also starred Sheree North, Vincent Price and John Carradine.

These pages: Elvis played the character of Walter Hale, the manager of a chautauqua company of actors and entertainers touring the Midwest in the 1920s, in *The Trouble with Girls.*

Above right: Elvis leaves the Philadelphia Hilton with (from left to right) Jerry Schilling, Joe Esposito, Red West and Dick Grob, 23 June 1974. Elvis's father Vernon follows along behind.
Above left: Elvis playing football in *The Trouble With Girls.*
Below: The King live on stage in the 1970s.
Right: Elvis in action during the 1968 NBC TV special.
Overleaf: Elvis meets the Press the day after his 31 July 1969 comeback concert at the International Hotel in Las Vegas.

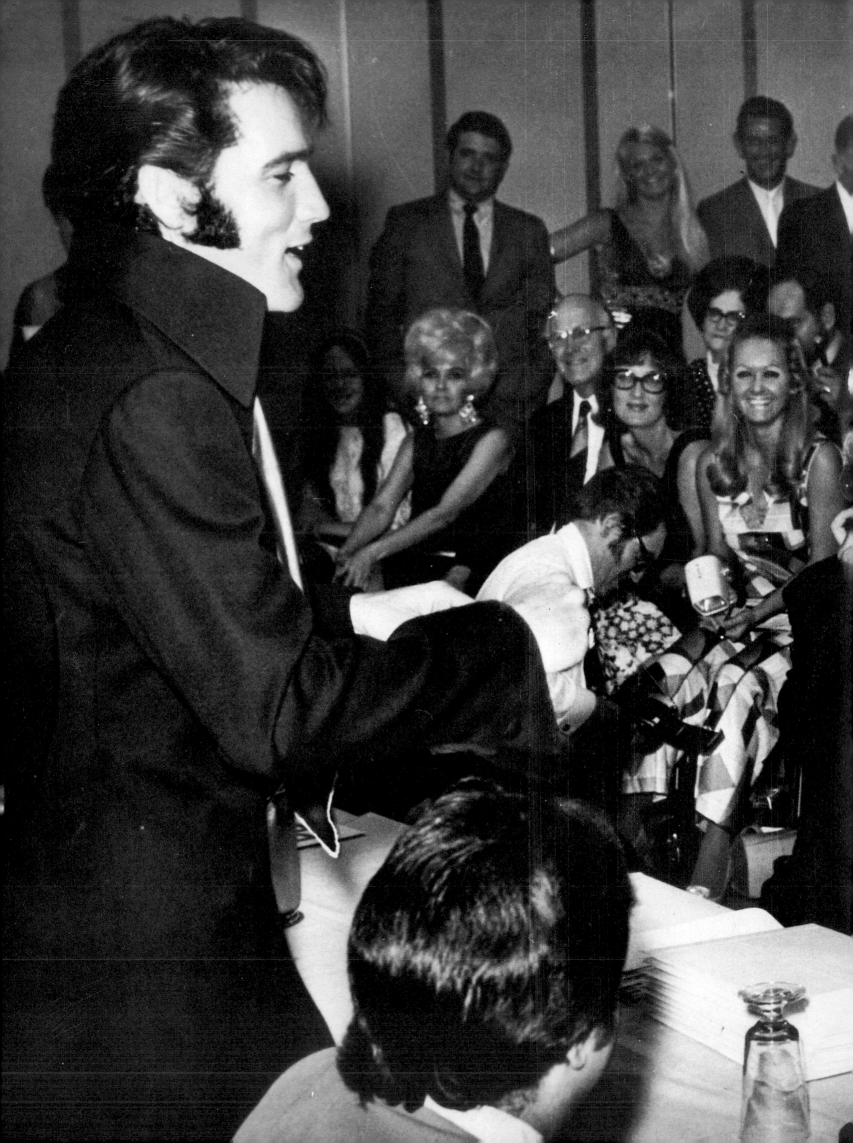

Previous pages: A series of photographs taken in the latter half of his long career.
Above: Elvis strums a song during a studio session in the early 1970s.
Right: A wistful look on the face of the King.
Far right: Elvis filmed during the 1968 TV special. Although filmed in the summer of that year, it was not broadcast until 3 December.

Above, left and below:
Elvis in *Charro*, a film that
marked the culmination of
the acting experience
gained by the King over the
past decade or so.
Opposite: A Change of

Habit, released by NBC-
Universal in January 1970,
saw Elvis star alongside
Mary Tyler Moore. Elvis
played Dr John Carpenter,
the head of a clinic in a
Puerto Rican neighborhood.

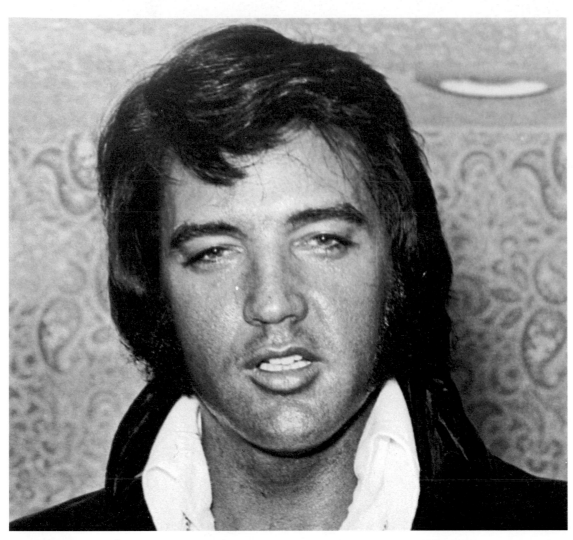

Far left: Elvis pictured in June 1972 during a Press conference in New York City prior to three concerts at Madison Square Garden.
Left: Elvis backstage at Las Vegas's Riviera Hotel in 1972.
Below: Elvis's fiancée Ginger Alden (*left*) and her mother Jo Alden during the investigation into the case against Dr George Nichopolous in 1981; his medical licence was suspended for over-prescribing drugs to Elvis and other clients.
Overleaf: A selection of pictures that capture the magic of the King at his finest.

Far left: Elvis on stage in 1973 performing his 'Aloha From Hawaii' show. It reached an estimated 500 million fans around the world.
Above: Elvis is escorted from a performance in the 1970s.
Right: The commitment of a truly professional performer is evident in this shot taken during the 1973 Hawaiian concert.

Elvis's live performances in the late '60s gave him a new lease of life. After nearly a decade of 'formula' movies he said 'I only feel really alive when I'm in front of my audience'; live concerts provided a new challenge.

Elvis and Priscilla divorced in 1973, and although they shared custody of Lisa Marie, their daughter was raised mainly by her mother. Elvis's last serious relationship was with Ginger Alden (*far right*).

Right: A stricken fan clutches a newspaper with the unbelievable news, 17 August 1977.

'Life was pretty good, all except them last years. Then it got so I don't think he had a peaceful day' – Vester Presley, Elvis's uncle. The King died at his beloved Graceland. Tributes poured in from around the world, thousands of mourners filed past his coffin, and August 18th, the day of his funeral, was declared a day of mourning in Tennessee.

Mourners brought Memphis to a standstill on the day of Elvis's funeral. So crowded were the streets that it took the funeral cortege over an hour to travel the three miles between Graceland and the cemetery.

Above: Elvis was finally laid to rest in the Meditation Garden at Graceland. Half a million people visit the house and the grave every year.

Graceland is held in trust for Lisa Marie until her 25th birthday. At present it is administered as a museum with Elvis's stage suits, records and cars on show. The Presley legend is big business, and Graceland is now the most recognizable private home in the US after the White House.

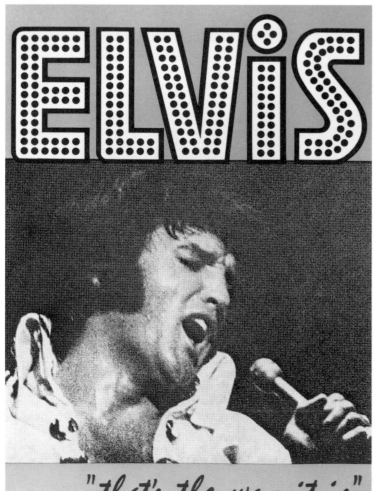

"that's the way it is."

Thirteen years after his death Elvis remains immensely profitable: in 1989 the estate received $15 million from royalties. As many as 5000 fans a day tour the house, curious to see how the King lived.

U.S.A. '85
Elvis Presley
Memorial Tour
& Florida
with the Official Elvis Presley Fan Club

FANCLUBCARD

ELVIS
PRESLEY FAN CLUB

EXPIRES END

ELVIS

FOR CONDITIONS SEE OVER

EPILOGUE

Elvis Prelsey died on 16 August 1977. He was found fully-clothed face-down on his bathroom floor, and despite frantic efforts to revive him, he was prounounced dead at 4pm. The medical examiner's report concluded 'Basically it was a natural death. The precise cause of death may never be discovered.'

Within hours, thousands of bereft fans began gathering outside Graceland, hoping against hope that the rumors were untrue. By the next day, when the King returned to Graceland for the last time, over 80,000 people struggled down a packed Elvis Presley Boulevard to pay their respects. Tributes poured in from around the world; fellow singers and actors, politicians and fans all seemed anxious to record their grief and to express a debt of gratitude to Elvis. 'I think part of America died when Elvis passed away,' said his old colleague Carl Perkins, and President Jimmy Carter spoke for

millions when he said 'Elvis may be gone but his legend will be with us for a long time to come.'

On the day of the funeral a 16-car motorcade took Elvis from Graceland to the cemetery along a three-mile route lined by fans. His final resting place is in the Meditation Garden at Graceland.

Whatever may be written about the way Elvis lived, no-one can underestimate the effect of the man's music. In the mid-1950s Elvis Presley *was* rock'n'roll, and most of the great stars who followed cited Elvis as their inspiration. Many years after his death, Elvis still seems as popular as ever; the Presley estate receives several million dollars every year from the sales of records and memorabilia, and half a million fans flood the music gates at Graceland and file reverently around the house. The King may be gone, but his music, films and the devotion of his fans ensure that the legend of Elvis Presley will never die.

'He was admired not only as an entertainer, but as the great humanitarian that he was, for his generosity and his kind feelings for his fellow man. He became a living legend in his own time earning the respect of milions:' The inscription on Elvis's tomb stone.

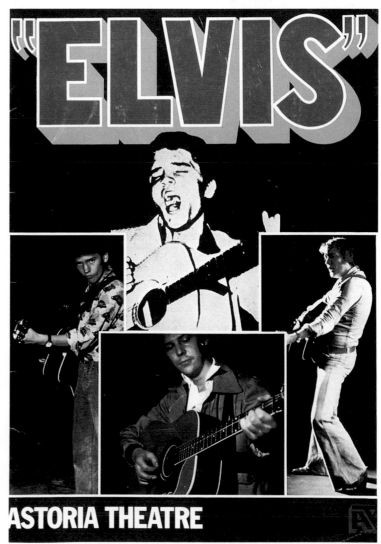

ASTORIA THEATRE

INDEX

Acknowledgments

The author and publisher would like to thank Mike Rose, Sue Casebourne and David Eldred for designing this book; Helen Dawson for preparing the index; Simon Gregory for editorial advice; Veronica Price and Nicki Giles in the production department, and Judith Millidge for editing it. We would also like the thank the following agencies for supplying the pictures on the pages noted below.

American Graphic System: pages 19 (top), 29 (top right), 30 (bottom), 33, 36 (both), 48 (top & right), 52 (top right), 62 (bottom left), 65 (top), 67 (top two), 68 (top two), 76 (bottom), 80 (bottom & right), 87 (top), 99, 100, (both), 101 (both), 102 (all three), 103, 120 (both), 121 (top), 146 (left), 151 (bottom), 185 (top), 222 (bottom), 223, 228 (bottom), 229 (bottom), 230 (bottom), 236 (bottom two), 237 (top), 238 (bottom), 279, 287 (bottom), 292 (top two)

British Film Institute: pages 7, 8 (both), 9 (top), 12 (both), 13 (all three), 14 (bottom two), 16 (all three), 17 (top), 18 (all three), 21, 22 (bottom right), 26, 29 (top), 36 (top two), 37, 46 (top two), 52 (bottom left), 63, 64 (both), 65 (bottom two), 66, 67 (bottom), 68 (bottom), 72 (both), 73, 74 (both), 75, 76 (top), 77 (both), 78 (both), 82 (top two), 83 (both), 84 (both), 85 (top two), 86 (top), 87 (bottom), 106-113, 124-126, 128 (all three), 130-135, 137 (top & left), 142-144, 145 (bottom), 146 (top two), 147, 148, 149 (top & left), 150 (all three), 151 (top), 152-160, 162-163, 166-168, 169 (top & left), 170-178, 179 (top right), 180-183, 184 (bottom), 185 (top two). 186-210, 211 (top), 212-218, 220-221, 224-225, 229 (top right), 241-243, 244 (right two), 252 (bottom two), 253 (all three), 256-271, 272 (bottom), 280 (right & bottom), 281 (all five)

Graceland Estate: pages 232, 233 (top), 240 (bottom), 296 (bottom two), 297 (bottom), 298 (top)

Pictorial Press: pages 1, 2, 5, 6, 10 (bottom), 11, 15, 20, 22 (left two), 32 (top), 34-35, 38-39, 41-43, 44 (four), 45, 47 (both), 54-59, 62 (top), 88, 89 (top), 94, 96 (bottom), 98 (top two), 104 (top right & bottom left), 114 (bottom & left), 115, 119, 122-123, 127, 129, 136, 137 (right), 138 (bottom left), 140-141, 161, 164-165, 169 (bottom right), 179 (bottom), 219, 222 (top two), 226 (both), 230 (top left), 231, 233 (bottom), 234, 235 (center, top, right), 238 (top), 246-249, 254 (three), 255 (three), 272 (top two), 273, 276, 277 (top two), 278 (top two), 280 (top left), 282, 284 (all three), 285, 287 (top), 288 (both), 289, 292 (bottom), 296 (top two), 297 (three), 300 (top & right), 301 (top), 304

UPI/Bettmann Archive: pages 9 (bottom), 17 (bottom),

19 (bottom two), 22 (top right), 23-25, 27, 28, 29 (bottom right), 31, 32 (bottom), 40, 44 (top left), 50-51, 53, 60, 61 (bottom right), 69-71, 79, 80 (top left), 81, 82 (bottom left), 85 (right), 86 (bottom), 89 (bottom), 90-93, 95 (all three), 96 (top), 97, 98 (bottom two), 104 (top left, bottom right), 105, 114 (top right), 116 (both), 117, 118, 139, 145 (top), 184 (top), 227 (bottom), 228 (top), 229 (top left), 235 (left, top & bottom), 237 (bottom), 239, 240 (top right), 251, 254 (bottom left), 274-275, 277 (bottom two), 278 (bottom), 283 (both), 286, 290 (all three), 291, 293, 294, 295, 301 (bottom right)

Vintage Magazine Company: pages 10 (top), 46 (bottom), 49 (both), 82 (top right), 211 (bottom), 227 (top two), 236 (top left), 245, 255 (top left), 298 (bottom left), 299 (both), 300 (bottom left), 301 (bottom left)